T0145275

Grandma Edie's ABC Book

Edith Pye

GRANDMA EDIE'S ABC BOOK

iUniverse books may be ordered through booksellers or by contacting:

iUniverse
1663 Liberty Drive
Bloomington, IN 47403
www.iuniverse.com
1-800-Authors (1-800-288-4677)

ISBN: 978-1-5320-5623-9 (sc)
ISBN: 978-1-5320-5624-6 (e)

Library of Congress Control Number: 2018909743

Print information available on the last page.

iUniverse rev. date: 08/17/2018

I am an apple, so round and sweet; I am loved by many. So taste and eat.

B

I am a box to put your toys in; when you obey, you are mama's little friend.

I am a car. My color is blue; I am put together with hands and glue.

D

I am a duck, in water I play; I come out to shake, go back in another day.

E

I am an elephant, so large and gray; I eat a lot of vegetables and greens every day.

I am a flower. On my petal sits a bee; when the wind blows, the bee will flee.

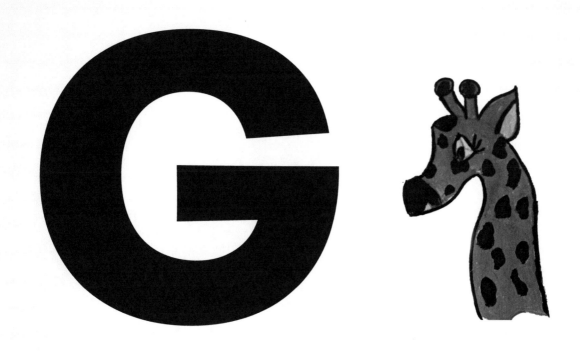

I am a giraffe, so tall and thin;
my neck is long. I eat with a silly
grin.

I am a house, and not a barn. They painted me red. I was built on a farm.

I am an iron, I get very hot. Do not touch me, or you will hurt a lot.

I am a jet, and I can fly; lots of people wave to me goodbye.

I am a kitten, so soft and sweet;
my tail is fluffy. I have small feet.

I am a lamp. I sit by your bed, day and night; to chase away the dark and give you light.

I am a monkey, born in a zoo. Swinging on a tree, that's what I love to do.

I am a number; you need to count with me. It's easy, just 1 2 3.

I am an octopus. I have 8 arms, and look very odd; sometimes I have to run from a fishing rod.

P

I am a pony that you can ride;
hold on tight, I may run and hide.

I am a quilt your mama made for you. Every stitch is made with love; something old and something new.

I am a rabbit, fat and round as you can see. I love carrots and they are good for me.

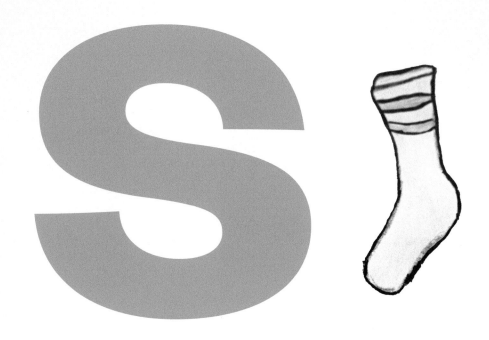

I am a sock. I fit in your shoe; try me on, and you will know what to do.

T

I am a top. I go round and round;
I play music when you sit me
down.

I am an umbrella, a special little thing. If you use me right, I will keep you from the rain.

I am a vest; a friend when you swim. I keep you safe where you are going, and back where you have been.

I am a wagon, for children to ride. I am large enough for a friend to sit by your side.

I am a Xenops; a bird with a beautiful song. I live in the rain forest; that is where I belong.

I am a yo-yo. My shape is round;
hold my string, I will go up and
down.

I am a zoo, for animals to stay; they can scream, run, play and jump all day.

This book is dedicated to all my grandchildren and great grandchildren; to remind them how much I love them, and the joy they bring to me, and to always remember their Grandma Edie.

- Grandma

To all my grandchildren;

Garfield and Brooklyn Chambers

Brianna and Nate Bertram

Elijah and Faith Chambers

Merle and Andrea Chambers

Jessica Marlene Pierce

Christen Faith Chambers

Gregory McLendon Chambers

Andrew Patrick Pierce

Natalie and Canon Xiong

Tristan Pierce Chambers

John Keith Chambers

Holly Rebecca Chambers

Garrison Reid Chambers

Carson Scott Shiflett

Anna Grace Keller

Robert "Brooks" Keller

And to all of my Great Grandchildren;

Kendall Mareen Smith

Penelope Elisabeth Chambers

Charlie Ann Chambers

Georgia Grace Bertram

Adrian Merle Chambers

Garfield Junior Chambers (5th)

Donna Mae Chambers

Canon Caspian Xiong

Steven Elijah Chambers

And a special thank you to my granddaughter Christen for her help with this book.

Printed in the United States
By Bookmasters